Three Hours

Three Hours

Sermons for Good Friday

Fleming Rutledge

William B. Eerdmans Publishing Company

Grand Rapids, Michigan

Wm. B. Eerdmans Publishing Co.
4035 Park East Court SE, Grand Rapids, Michigan 49546
www.eerdmans.com

28 27 26 25 24 23 22 21 20 19   1 2 3 4 5 6 7 8 9 10

ISBN 978-0-8028-7719-2

Library of Congress Cataloging-in-Publication Data

A catalog record for this book is available from the Library of Congress

The author and publisher gratefully acknowledge permission to reprint Joy Williams, "Wet," in *Ninety-nine Stories of God*. Copyright © 2016 by Joy Williams. Reprinted by permission of ICM Partners and Tin House Books.

In memory of my master teacher

Paul Louis Lehmann

Crux probat omnia

St. Thomas Fifth Avenue in New York City is one of very few Episcopal churches remaining in the United States that still offers a full three hours of preaching, interspersed with music and prayers, for the noon-to-three service of worship on Good Friday. It was a great honor to be invited to give these sermons on that day in 2018. They are reproduced here almost exactly as they were preached.

For me, this occasion felt like a culmination of all my preaching over the past forty-five years. I would like to think that there are many potential readers who will find these offerings helpful as they seek to understand more fully the nature of the sacrifice that God himself made in the person of his Son on Good Friday in Jerusalem two millennia ago. My earlier book, *The Crucifixion: Understanding the Death of Jesus Christ*, expounds this theme at length. I hope that this slim volume might encourage readers to further pursue the depths of the Scriptures concerning what Paul the Apostle called the heart of the Christian gospel: "Jesus Christ and him crucified."

If you would like to hear the sermons as originally preached, the webcast may be found at http://www.saint thomaschurch.org/calendar/events/worship/21936/the -three-hours-devotion#webcast. My thanks to Avery Griffin, Website Manager and Audio Engineer at Saint Thomas Church Fifth Avenue, for his work in making this webcast available.

For the most part, I have preferred to use the Revised Standard Version translation of the Bible, although in two or three places I have used an alternate English translation of a word in order to emphasize what I take to be the meaning of the original Greek. The RSV remains my standard because, while it modernizes the King James Version and corrects its mistakes, it preserves much of the KJV cadence that made that translation so uniquely powerful and memorable. I have used the KJV itself in the translations at the head of the chapters.

And there were also two others, malefactors, led with him to be put to death. And when they were come to the place, which is called Calvary, there they crucified him, and the malefactors, one on the right hand, and the other on the left. Then said Jesus, Father, forgive them; for they know not what they do. And they parted his raiment, and cast lots.

Luke 23:32–34

A s Jesus Christ was being nailed to the cross, he said, "Father, forgive them; for they know not what they do" (Luke 23:34). For whom, exactly, was he interceding? It was the Roman soldiers who were doing the immediate hands-on deed.[1] Or was he forgiving Caiaphas the high priest and his kangaroo court? Pontius Pilate, who washed his hands of him? Peter, who denied him three times? In any case, this saying sets forgiveness at the heart and center of Luke's passion narrative. But to what extent does Christian forgiveness extend to those who *know exactly* what they are doing? These are not easy questions.

I was struck by an article on the front page of "the failing *New York Times*" about six weeks ago.[2] It was about a

---

1. Certainly, the soldiers did not know what they were doing, although, according to Luke, when Jesus drew his last breath a centurion declared that Jesus was innocent.

2. This was a tip of the hat to a congregation of New Yorkers who were

defense attorney on a prominent case involving a terrorist.[3]
His name is Alaric Piette, a former Navy SEAL with only six
years' experience as a lawyer, and no experience at all with
a case involving the death penalty. He agrees with his critics
that he is unfit for his task, but it seems that the whole legal
team resigned from the case, and he was the only lawyer
willing to stay with it.

Lt. Piette's client is Abd al-Rahim al-Nashiri, a Saudi
Arabian accused of planning the bombing of the US de-
stroyer *Cole* in the year 2000. This is a person that almost
any American would assume deserved conviction and a
harsh penalty. The case is complicated, though, because he
was tortured for four years in a CIA black site and remains
profoundly traumatized. Here's what caught my attention
in the article. During Lt. Piette's last year at the Georgetown
Law School, he decided that he would not become a prose-
cutor as he had originally planned. He shifted his emphasis
to criminal defense. Raised Roman Catholic, he found that
representing destitute, often mentally ill clients enabled

---

well aware that President Donald J. Trump habitually referred to the newspa-
per in this way.

3. Dave Philipps, "Many Say He's the Least Qualified Lawyer Ever to
Lead a Guantánamo Case. He Agrees," *The New York Times*, February 5, 2018.

him to really understand the teachings of Jesus for the first time. He said, "It was the first time since [I left] the SEALs [that] I found something really meaningful. I was standing between a person and the system." Many of the members of the team that left the case expressed extreme disdain for Lt. Piette, but one of his professors at Georgetown displayed his photo in her ethics class as an example of "a courageous and ethical representation. . . . He's pretty gutsy. This legal train is in motion and he steps out in front to protect his client. I don't know that all lawyers would do that."

Let's assume that the accused Saudi man is indeed guilty of plotting the terrorist act. Is he deserving of a defense? Does he have "rights"? Our system teaches us to presume innocence until proven guilty, but what are guilt and innocence, ultimately, in the sight of God?

A few days ago I had lunch with three clergy friends and we discussed this matter. One of them described a poster he had seen in a pacifist church not long after American Special Forces ambushed and killed Osama bin Laden. The poster had an illustration of Jesus greeting and embracing Osama bin Laden. All four of us agreed that this was offensive, but we agreed also that it sharply raised the question of exactly how far Christian forgiveness should go and who should receive it. Did Osama bin Laden know what he was doing? Should only people who don't know what they are doing be forgiven? Did the young man with the AR-15 at the Stoneman Douglas High School know what he was doing?[4]

The book of Leviticus prescribes various religious sacrifices that should be made by people who have "unwittingly" broken the laws of God. Even if they "knew not" what they have done, they are judged guilty and must seek atonement. Significantly, there is no provision made in Leviticus for *deliberate* sin. Isn't that interesting? If you commit an "unwitting" offense, you have a remedy. But the person who commits sins "with a high hand," as we read in the book of Numbers, has no remedy, but will be "utterly cut off" from the community, and "his iniquity shall be upon him" (Numbers 15:30–31). We'll get back to "high-handed iniquity" shortly, but for now we'll just note that the basic idea in the sacrificial rituals of Leviticus is the idea that atonement for sin *costs something*. Something valuable has to be offered in restitution. The life of the animal sacrifice, and a sense of awe at the shedding of blood, represents this payment. This is what the book of Hebrews in the New Testament means

4. One of America's tragically frequent school shootings, this one in Parkland, Florida, had recently occurred.

when it says, "Without the shedding of blood there is no forgiveness of sins" (Hebrews 9:22). The blood represents the ultimate cost to the giver. There is something powerful here that grips us in spite of ourselves.[5] We are left, however, with the problem of the person who knows what he or she is doing.

I have often told a story about a man I knew in one of my former parishes. He was very well-educated and prominent in the community, but he was not at all self-important. I had no idea that he had been in the fabled Tenth Mountain Division during World War II, and I certainly didn't know that he had received the Silver Star until I went to a veterans' gathering and someone told me. I started oohing and aahing to the veteran about his Silver Star, but he cut me off. He said, crisply and definitively, "Nobody knows who deserves what." The more I have thought about that over the last twenty years, the more true it seems to me to be. An act of great courage performed by one person might be humanly impossible for another person with a different psychological makeup. Only God knows who deserves what.

5. The use of the phrase "blood of Christ" in the New Testament carries with it this sacrificial, atoning significance in a primordial sense; we cannot root out these connections even if we want to.

What about "high-handed iniquity"? What forces make a person deliberately do evil things? We know so little about this. Certainly people who mastermind terrorist acts are doing it with a high hand. But then so was the CIA acting with a high hand in setting up black sites to torture people. Torturing another person does profound damage to the soul of the one doing the torturing. Human justice is necessary for human life to exist, but human justice is exceedingly imperfect, and—here's the point—*it can never restore what was lost*. In speaking of God, we must seek other dimensions, because in certain cases, Christian forgiveness seems almost immoral.[6] The picture of Jesus embracing Osama bin Laden is a markedly superficial image of the nature of Christian forgiveness and the justice of our Creator. There is something missing from this image, and that is the righteousness of God.

For the apostle Paul, the righteousness of God was absolutely central. Paul's favorite word *justification* means the same thing as *righteousness* in Greek (and also in Hebrew). Paul says in Romans 4 that we are *justified by the blood of Jesus*. A better translation might be that we are *being made*

6. Christopher Hitchens pointed this out, and from his atheist perspective he may have been quite right.

righteous through Jesus' death on the cross. This is more comprehensive and more revolutionary than forgiveness by itself.

In Romans 5, Paul sums up the Christian message in words that everyone should know, whether you are a Christian or not, because this is the heart and soul of the Christian message and what the death of Christ means for every human being:

> While we were still helpless, at the right time Christ died for the *ungodly*. . . . God shows his love for us in that *while we were still sinners* Christ died for us. (Romans 5:6, 8)

And in Romans 4, Paul says the same thing in reference to Abraham. He explains that Abraham knew better than to trust in his own good works. Rather, he trusted in the God who justifies—wait for it—"the *ungodly*" (Romans 4:5).

Now every single religious idea the world has ever seen depends on a concept of becoming *more godly*—more religious, more spiritual. What would be the point of religion if not to make people godly? Here is where the Christian faith diverges from "religion," and here the gospel preached by the apostle Paul appears in its most radical form. God is the one who justifies the *un*godly.

The ungodly. Who are these ungodly people? We have only ungodly people here today. The ungodly people are you and me, along with Abraham and Isaac, Sarah and Rebekah, Peter and Paul, Mary and Martha. Paul couldn't have known that the great American gospel was going to be "God helps those who help themselves," but he couldn't have demolished it more succinctly than in these words: "While we were still helpless, Christ died for the ungodly."

There are elements of myself that are indefensible. There are elements of yourself that are indefensible. If you don't know that, you don't yet know the grace of God. If we don't understand our own defenselessness in the grip of Sin and Death, we do not yet know who it is who comes to us as the One who justifies the ungodly. Forgiveness needs to be understood in this way. *Forgiveness* is too weak a word for what God does. *Justification* is the word. It is not up to me or you to determine what God is going to do about Osama bin Laden. We can only say that God is able to do mighty works of making right what has been wrong. Never mind Osama bin Laden; God is going to make right what is wrong with *me*—how I look forward to that day! Justification means more than forgiveness. The forgiveness offered by one human being to another makes no sense in the case of "high-handed" sin. The only way we can think in terms of forgiveness in extreme cases is that God can and will make right all that has been wrong. Luke wrote a beautiful, luminous Gospel, but we need Paul to tell us that forgiveness alone is not enough. To be forgiven by God is to be *justified*: to be remade in the image of the new Adam, who is Jesus Christ, the great Defender of the defenseless.

In this sense, the defender of the ungodly in the earthly court of military justice is a reflection— a very dim and imperfect reflection, but a reflection nonetheless—of the justice of God.

"While we were still helpless, Christ died for the ungodly." We are guilty as hell, and the legal train is in motion, but the Son of God who will come to be the Judge of all the world has stepped out in front to protect us. If you understand this, you are already being remade by the sacrifice of Christ. This is the gospel. "God shows his love for us in that while we were *still sinners* Christ died for us."

We are going to sing the greatest of all Good Friday hymns. It's from the Evangelical Lutheran tradition, by Johann Heermann, who wrote many of the texts for Bach's chorales. As we sing it today, we will recognize ourselves in it. *We* are the ungodly for whom Christ died. We will recognize two things at once: we will recognize ourselves as guilty and condemned, and *at the same moment* we will recognize that we ourselves are the ones for whom Christ died—for he is the One who justifies the ungodly, the One who will incorporate us into himself and remake us after his own image in the company of all the saints, rejoicing with the Father who awaits us with arms flung wide at his overflowing banquet in the Kingdom of heaven.

Ah, holy Jesus, how hast thou offended,
That man to judge thee hath in hate pretended?
By foes derided, by thine own rejected,
O most afflicted.

Who was the guilty? Who brought this upon thee?
Alas, my treason, Jesus, hath undone thee.
'Twas I, Lord Jesus, I it was denied thee,
I crucified thee.

Lo, the Good Shepherd for the sheep is offered;
The slave hath sinnèd, and the Son hath suffered;

For our atonement, while we nothing heeded,
God interceded.

For me, kind Jesus, was thy incarnation,
Thy mortal sorrow, and thy life's oblation;
Thy death of anguish and thy bitter passion,
For my salvation.

Therefore, kind Jesus, since I cannot pay thee,
I do adore thee, and will ever pray thee,
Think on thy pity, and thy love unswerving,
Not my deserving.[7]

7. Hymn by Johann Heermann (1585–1647).

And one of the malefactors which were hanged railed on
him, saying, If thou be Christ, save thyself and us. But the
other answering rebuked him, saying, Dost not thou fear
God, seeing thou art in the same condemnation? . . . And
he said unto Jesus, Lord, remember me when thou comest
into thy kingdom. And Jesus said unto him, Verily I say unto
thee, Today shalt thou be with me in paradise.

Luke 23:39–43

The first two sayings from the cross are from the Gospel of Luke, and also the last one. In all my many years of preaching on Good Friday I've come to believe that we are enriched by seeing the different ways in which the four evangelists—Matthew, Mark, Luke, and John—tell the story of Jesus. Each of them has certain key features in common, but at the same time each one has a special point of view, and we don't want simply to conflate them as if they were all the same. In this saying from Luke's Gospel, the two—Luke and John—show a similarity: Jesus is pinned to an instrument of torture, completely helpless, at the mercy of sadistic torturers and mocking passersby, and yet he is reigning from the cross as a King.

A King, and yet crucified between two thieves. The traditional word is *thief*, but that's misleading. This is not Jean Valjean stealing a loaf of bread. These are bandits, brigands—lawless, full-time professionals who were a serious threat to the famous Roman rule of order. Crucifixion was the supreme penalty (*summum supplicium*, Cicero called it) for a particular type of criminal, guilty of the impermissible offense of sedition (rebellious disorder, in the archaic sense of the word). These men have often been described as "common criminals," but that's not quite right. The Romans didn't waste their time crucifying small-timers. These two men were a serious threat to the system. So they've been tried by the Romans and condemned by their laws, presumably with justification, for one of them actually admits that he was justly convicted for being an insurrectionist, for "perverting the people"—the term used by Pontius Pilate (Luke 23:14).

So that's what crucifixion was for—a method of displaying people in the most cruel circumstances possible, to demonstrate publicly the power of the empire not just to kill, but to dehumanize—and by so doing, to deter anyone who dared to think of defying Caesar. Talk about a deterrent! Cruel, inhuman, public, and prolonged torture, that's what it was. And the message was, this will happen to you, too, if you dare to raise your hand against the emperor.

So here are these three men, pinned up on crosses like insects, exposed to the mockery of the passersby—for crucifixion was a ritual of humiliation. It's almost impossible for us to imagine, really, but in Roman times everyone had seen crucifixions, so it wasn't necessary for the evangelists to go into detail. In addition to the physical pain and the shame of naked exposure, the victim was deliberately dehumanized to the point of being unrecognizable. A message was being sent: this object that you see before you is displayed here specifically so that you can vent your most sadistic and inhuman impulses. You can say and do anything you want to these wretches; you have the permission of the emperor. And we may be sure, the people played their roles with gusto—as at any public lynching. It's important that we understand the extreme shaming that the Son of God underwent on the cross.

So here are these two brigands on either side of Jesus. One of them is defiant even in his utter defenselessness. Here is Luke's account:

> One of the criminals who were hanged railed at him, saying, "Are you not the Christ? Save yourself and us!" But the other rebuked him, saying, "Do you not

fear God, since you are under the same sentence
of condemnation? And we indeed justly; for we
are receiving the due reward of our deeds; but this
man has done nothing wrong." And he said, "Jesus,
remember me when you come into your kingdom."
(Luke 23:39–42)

"Remember me when you come into your kingdom."
What made him think that Jesus had a kingdom? What and
how, exactly, did he surmise? Perhaps he was able to read
the inscription that Pilate put over Jesus' head, "The King of
the Jews." He seems to have received insight into the hidden
power of God. Thus also you and I are placed today in the
position of beholding Jesus on the cross and searching for
the answer, whether he is or is not the Lord of a Kingdom.
The convicted brigand, whatever or however he glimpsed
the truth, made the essential move: he placed himself in the
hands of Jesus. Think of that! Giving oneself into the care
of a man who has no power even to move his own pinioned
hands, a helpless victim of the great Roman Empire that
held sway throughout the known world, a degraded, naked,
bloodied, fouled, reviled castoff about to become a corpse.
Somehow seeing beyond all that, the convicted criminal

next to him confesses him as a King. "Jesus, remember me when you come into your kingdom."

Think of these words as your own words in your own ultimate situation. Think of these words spoken by a felon, a man you would be terrified of if you met him on the road, and of the extraordinary circumstances of his becoming the one to give you the words of insight in your greatest extremity: "Lord, remember *me* when you come into your kingdom." These can be our words, at any moment of crisis in our own lives. For the central idea here is the power of Jesus to save, to rescue, to deliver. The paradox is that of his power precisely in his powerlessness. We need to stop and envision this: he is a prisoner of his own body. The weight of his body is killing him. The only power left to him is the power of his Word.

And Jesus said to the condemned man hanging next to him, "Truly, I say to you, today you will be with me in Paradise" (Luke 23:43).

It's important not to lose focus here. So much unhelpful speculation has gone into these words. People ask things like, Is this proof that we go directly to heaven when we die? Did Jesus go to heaven that very day, before the resurrection even, bringing the bandit along with him? These are not important questions for Luke, and they should not be important to us either.

Let's think instead about the nature of what Jesus might mean by paradise. You and I know that there are a thousand and one concepts of paradise. Usually it's a garden of some sort. Or it's up in the sky with clouds and angels. We've all heard about the suicide bombers who are promised seventy-two virgins in paradise (apparently a misreading of the Qur'an). Most people think of paradise as reunion with their loved ones, including their beloved pets. Karl Barth was once asked if we would be with our loved ones in heaven. He replied, "Not only our loved ones!"

I make a point of visiting cemeteries and studying the gravestones, sometimes in my native Virginia, mostly in New England. You can get a sense of what people think paradise might be. The nineteenth-century stones often have Bible verses on them, or lines from poems. In the twentieth century they become more plain, with just the names and dates. In recent years there's been a decided trend toward illustration. Favorite motifs on more recent stones are flowers, of course, and military insignia, but also sailboats, fishing scenes, golf courses (I'm not making this up). I haven't seen any NRA motifs, but I'm sure they're out

there . . . some of you may remember that good Episcopa-
lian, Charlton Heston, saying that he was going to die with
his rifle in his hand.

All this wishful thinking about paradise is swept away
by what Jesus says from the cross. The sentence contains the
secret in just two words. Listen again: "Today you will be
with me in Paradise." The two important words are not "in
Paradise." The two important words are "with me." That's
the key. Paradise is where Jesus is, and being in paradise
is being with him. The Bible verse on my grandparents'
gravestone in Virginia is from Psalm 16:11. It reads, "In thy
presence is fulness of joy." Just to be in the presence of Jesus
forever, that is paradise. Truly to know Jesus is to know that
his love infinitely exceeds any human love that we have ever
known, and his love is able to deliver even at the door of
death. Our Savior is One who is able to promise his eternal
company in heaven with God to a man dying alongside him
on an instrument of torture.

Could that malefactor have known that he would be the
first person to arrive with Jesus at the gates of the Kingdom
of heaven? The Epistle to the Hebrews says that Jesus is the
first member of the resurrection of the dead. He is the pio-
neer (Hebrews 12:2), but *with him* he will bring all who put

their trust in him. And the first one for whom he does that at the very gate of death is, quite simply, a wretch. Amazing grace that saved a wretch like this man! Amazing grace that saved a wretch like me!

My grandparents' gravestone inscription meant little to me when I was young. It was just words on a piece of granite. But my grandmother is the one who led me into the world of the Bible. She used to have me over to spend the night, and while I was having a bath in some sort of marvellous lavender water, she read to me from the King James Version. She died when I was eight years old, but she had done her work. The Bible and the lavender water blended into one another and became "living water." Over the decades, especially as the verse from the psalm began to grow in my consciousness, I began to understand the depth of her knowledge and love of the Lord. It's strange—I think she may have been a difficult person in some ways—but what a perfect example of the way God uses us in spite of ourselves. Wherever she is now, whatever paradise might be in its details, it is "with him." *In his presence* is fullness of joy. "Lord, remember me when you come into your kingdom."

THIRD SERMON

When Jesus therefore saw his mother, and the disciple standing by, whom he loved, he saith unto his mother, Woman, behold thy son! Then saith he to the disciple, Behold thy mother! And from that hour that disciple took her unto his own home.

John 19:26–27

The day of Jesus' crucifixion was not—I am sorry to disappoint anyone—*was not* the first Mother's Day. It was something infinitely more embracing, more universal, more radical. One of our best interpreters of the Gospel of John writes of this very simply: "At the time of the Lord's death, a new family is brought into being."[1] This, above all, was and is the goal of his life, his death, and his resurrection: to bind himself to a united fellowship of believers with whom he would abide forever. The New Testament calls this new family the *ecclesia*, the church. We aren't singing it today, but one of our popular hymns says it perfectly: "The church's one foundation is Jesus Christ her Lord. / She is his new creation, by water and the Word."[2]

And yet many of us don't understand what is happening on Good Friday. We Americans tend to be a sentimen-

1. E. C. Hoskyns, *The Fourth Gospel* (1947), 530.
2. Hymn by Samuel John Stone (1839–1900).

tal people. This makes it difficult for us to look directly
into the horror, shame, and degradation of a death by
crucifixion. In the case of this particular saying from the
cross, our tendency toward sentimentality causes us to
prefer the idea that this saying of our Lord on the cross is
about taking good care of your mother. I am a mother, and
I definitely want to be taken care of! But this is not what
the Fourth Evangelist, John, wants us to understand. In
the Fourth Gospel, the mother of our Lord plays a quite
different role.

Over here on my right, in the chapel in the side aisle,
there's a beautiful, unusual altarpiece. It depicts one of
John's memorable stories, the marriage feast at Cana. This
is the scene where Jesus says to his mother, "Woman,
what have you to do with me? My hour is not yet come"
(John 2:4). In English, this sounds very rude. In Greek it
is more respectful, but we notice that Jesus does not call
her "Mother," and she responds to him not as his mother,
but as one of his followers—one who is beginning to
have a glimmering of an idea about who he is. She says
to the servant, "Whatever he tells you, do it" (v. 5). She
is learning to be his disciple. That's what Mary represents
in the Gospel of John. She does not appear again in the

Fourth Gospel—except in passing and in company with others—until his hour actually *does* come and he is crucified.

From the cross, once again Jesus calls her "woman" rather than "Mother." Her identity as Jesus' mother is not important to John. It's striking that John never uses the name Mary for Jesus' mother. The Marys in his Gospel are those other true disciples, Mary of Bethany and Mary Magdalene. In fact, it's remarkable how rarely the mother of Jesus is called Mary at all in the New Testament, except in those famous first chapters in Luke—the nativity story. As the New Testament presents her, when her son enters upon his ministry, she becomes a follower as others do, and like those others, she is a beloved member of the new family that comes into being through the power of Christ's death. In John's Gospel, she stands out as a particularly faithful disciple, one who follows Jesus through his ministry from the beginning even to its ghastly end at Golgotha. So, when he speaks to her and to the beloved disciple (traditionally John himself) from the cross, he is giving two unrelated believers to one another. He gives his mother to him and him to her, in a completely new kinship that infinitely transcends blood kinship.

The evangelist tells us that the beloved disciple takes the mother of Jesus to his own home "from that hour." It's of great significance that John uses the phrase "that hour." This doesn't mean that John and Mary took off for John's house right that minute. The idea of "the hour" is the heart and center of the Fourth Gospel; John has shaped his whole narrative around it. Throughout, Jesus speaks of his hour— "My hour is not yet come," and then finally, the day after Palm Sunday, he declares, "my hour has come" (John 17:1). For John, it's the turning point in the Lord's earthly life. The Lord's passion is about to begin.

What initiates Jesus' declaration? The moment when Jesus proclaims that his hour has come is the moment when, for the first time, a group of Gentiles comes to seek him out. They come to the disciple Philip and say to him, "Sir, we wish to see Jesus" (John 12:21). This event—the arrival of the Gentiles—is the inaugural event of Jesus' "hour," the hour of crucifixion, of Jesus being "lifted up" as he said he would be—"when I am lifted up from the earth, [I] will draw all [humanity] to myself" (John 12:32). Pilate, not knowing what he is doing, orders an inscription to be nailed up on Jesus' cross: "The King of the Jews." It is written— listen to this—written in Hebrew, Latin, and Greek (John

19:20). Do you see? Hebrew is the language of the Jewish nation, but now—in this "hour" of crucifixion—the King of the Jews is revealed as the King of the empire, the true Ruler of the world and all the people in it. This is the hour of the remaking of the *kosmos* and the reconciliation of human relationships.

And at the same time that his universal kingship is announced, Jesus turns his failing eyesight down to the people standing on the trash-strewn ground covered with blood and human waste and gives these two disciples to one another. These two who remain at the cross represent to us the beginning of the church in the moment of her Lord's degradation and suffering unto death. Again the hymn: "The church's one foundation is Jesus Christ her Lord . . . with his own blood he bought her and for her life he died."[3]

Taking the Gospel and the Epistles of John together, no writings in the New Testament are more concerned with the church than John. You wouldn't necessarily notice this, however, if you read the Gospel without looking for it. Our typical American individualism tends always to

3. Hymn by Samuel John Stone (1839–1900).

focus on the single, supposedly autonomous person, so we typically read the Bible through that lens. And it's true that for the first two-thirds of the Gospel, John features a striking number of personal, intimate conversations between Jesus and single individuals: the Samaritan woman, Nicodemus, the man born blind, Thomas, Martha of Bethany, Mary Magdalene. These stories stand out because they are beautifully crafted by John, a master dramatist. So, most people tend to read the Fourth Gospel that way. But the overwhelming emphasis in John is not on individuals, but on the organic connection that Jesus creates among those who put their trust in him. This theme reaches its apex in chapters 15 and 16, during the last hours of his life on earth, when he teaches, "I am the vine, you are the branches" (John 15:5).

There is no other way to be a disciple of Jesus than to be in communion with other disciples of Jesus. Why do you suppose the Lord didn't separate out each one of his followers, stand us up separately, pronounce us each a unique individual, and then bid us go off and create ourselves? He did the opposite; instead of making us *independent* and *self-centered*, he makes us *mutually interdependent* and *other-directed*. The night before he died, he washed his disciples' feet (John 13:1–20). He told them, "A new commandment I give to you, that you love one another even as I have loved you. . . . By this all men will know that you are my disciples, if you have love for one another" (John 13:34–35). And he prayed long and earnestly for them, the long "high-priestly" prayer of chapter 17: "Holy Father, keep them in thy name, which thou hast given me, that they may be one, even as [you and I] are one" (John 17:11).

The love that breaks down barriers, the love that "endures all things" (1 Corinthians 13:7), the love that forgets self and focuses entirely on the well-being of the beloved community—that is the love of the Father and the Son for each other and the love of the Son for us. This is not abstract. It is worked out in self-giving. But the love that Christ enacts and commands for his followers cannot be enacted in isolation. A young man who said, "Jesus and me, we've got our own thing goin' on" is sadly lacking in his understanding of what it means to abide in Jesus. Dorothy Day, the revered Catholic writer and activist, said repeatedly, "You can't practice love without community." As many analysts have lamented, our culture is in danger of losing this sense of community. I read something interesting in two different sources recently. People who do studies

33

of marriages have learned that married couples thrive best when they get together frequently with friends. The much-recommended "date night," one on one, is apparently not as therapeutic as a couple gathering with others. After nearly sixty years of marriage, I can speak to this: my husband and I thrive when we have guests—any guests, but we flourish particularly when we have guests who also know and love the Lord.

A beloved British play called *Journey's End*, about soldiers in World War I, has recently been made into a film. It last appeared live on Broadway in 2007. It's an ensemble play with several actors and no stars. Each actor has his own individuality, but each has more or less the same time on stage and each is equally important to the whole. There was an interview with the actors in the 2007 production. Here's what one of them said: "[Our director] said again and again that everything you do onstage is for someone else, it's never about you. *That was such a wonderful thing to think of.*"[4] Isn't that remarkable? This culture of ours is so focused on thinking about our

4. Melena Ryzik, "A Regiment of Actors Falls In, Night After Night," interview of cast of *Journey's End*, *The New York Times*, March 13, 2007. Emphasis added.

own selves. "My time, my space, myself"—that's just one advertising slogan out of so many. We are urged on a daily basis to be good to ourselves, develop ourselves, believe in ourselves, and yet here is this actor saying how wonderful it is to think of participating in something that was never about you, always for the good of the whole. That's the church when it's working the way it's supposed to. This is why Cyprian of Carthage said eighteen hundred years ago, "You cannot have God as your Father unless you have the Church as your mother."[5]

Another interview that struck me was with the famous contemporary artist Frank Stella. His latest work had just been exhibited to great acclaim. Yet he "did not seem to feel any pressure to blow the horn for his new work." He said, "Making art, for me, is the opportunity to be free of one's own identity. It's not about finding one's identity, no matter what the psychologists say. It's about losing one's identity. I want to make something great that applies to everyone. Then I myself can be submerged."[6]

5. Cyprian of Carthage, *On the Unity of the Church* 6.

6. "Critic's Notebook: Frank Stella Builds a Landmark Out of Romanticism and Steel; A Monumental Sculpture Is Headed for Washington," *New York Times*, May 17, 2001.

When the community that Christ died for is working the way it's supposed to, that is what is going on. It's hard, sometimes, to put this across, because it's so easy to dismiss the church out of hand. The church can break your heart with its sin. It's broken my heart a few times. Every day brings some new revelation about the awful things that have been done by the church. It's much easier to say, as many do, I can be a Christian without the church. But this is to renounce a most basic and fundamental message of Jesus throughout his ministry, and, as John dramatizes it, it is shown forth most of all from the cross, in Jesus' death. He is giving you to me and me to you. The disciples of Christ today as two thousand years ago are drawn together in mutual love of our Lord.

At the end of this service, those of you who are still here at the foot of the cross will leave the church in silence. The shock of walking out into the heedless throngs on Fifth Avenue is great, I have found. "Is it nothing to you, all you who pass by? Behold and see if there be any sorrow like [unto his] sorrow" (Lamentations 1:12). When you walk out, no one will speak to you, but something has happened to you in these three hours. For all its sins, though they be many, the church is still the Body of Christ himself.

You are loved by our Lord. There is no limit to the love of Christ which overcomes the sin within his Body. Please come back.

Now from the sixth hour there was darkness over all the land unto the ninth hour. And about the ninth hour Jesus cried with a loud voice, saying, Eli, Eli, lama sabachthani? that is to say, My God, my God, why hast thou forsaken me?

Matthew 27:45–46

As I've been pointing out to those who were here from the beginning, we have four different Gospel books that tell the story of Jesus from four different points of view. It's the same story, but the four books are not all alike. We learn different things about the crucifixion from the different Gospels. Matthew and Mark are the most similar, and one of the most striking similarities is that in Matthew and Mark, Jesus dies alone and abandoned. In Luke and John, there are a few disciples who remain—a few women and the beloved disciple usually identified as John. In order to understand Good Friday we need to be able to hold two pictures in our minds, just as artists over the centuries have painted the crucifixion in two ways, both of them truthful to the biblical record: one type of image shows the cross with John and Mary the mother of Jesus standing by, and the second shows Jesus on the cross alone in the dark.

Alone in the dark. I along with many others have been shattered by some recent news concerning a member of a congregation I used to be part of. I'm going to call him Bruce, although that was not his real name. He was very intelligent and had graduated from a famous university, but he seemed alone in the world. He had no family anywhere nearby. He was known to suffer from depression, and it was getting worse. He was in the grip of some alienating affliction. He spoke of this to a number of people over many months. A few weeks ago he jumped out of his apartment window to his death.

The condition of hopelessness is profoundly challenging for the church. Hopelessness drives people to suicide. Hopelessness can also be called *despair*. The word *despair* in Latin is *de sperare*, precisely meaning "without hope," to give up hope. Despair is the opposite of Christian faith, because the hope we have in the faithfulness of Jesus Christ is invincible. What then do we say when someone from our Christian community loses hope to such a degree that he destroys himself?

On the cross, Jesus Christ appears to have experienced the condition of hopelessness. "My God, my God, why have you forsaken me?" (Matthew 27:46; Mark 15:34).

During his life, Jesus always referred to God as his Father. In Luke's Gospel he prays twice to God as Father from the cross, but in Mark and Matthew his only prayer is a despairing cry to a more impersonal "God." There is nothing in either of those Gospels to soften the desolation of his situation. It is his only "word from the cross" in either one. Because this cry of dereliction, so called, is so difficult to think about and absorb, we tend to flee to the softer sayings in Luke's Gospel. On Good Friday, we are summoned to place special focus on the apparent sense of abandonment that Mark and Matthew place at the heart of their passion narratives.

About a year ago, I ran into Bruce at a church conference here in the city. There were a lot of people buzzing around, lots of social interaction. He seemed alone in the crowd. He came up to me and asked if I could meet him later that day for coffee. I apologized and said no, that I was tied up with commitments—which was true, that particular day. He said, with a little smile, "Well, maybe another time." Looking back, I think we both knew that there was not going to be another time. I don't live in Manhattan anymore, and I am somewhat overwhelmed with the details of my own life. That day was the last time I saw Bruce.

I have replayed this scene a hundred times in my mind since I heard the news of his death. Why didn't I call him back to set another date? Why didn't I try to make sure there was a group of people to keep a watch on him? Why didn't I find out what floor he lived on? Why didn't I at least give him the number of a suicide-prevention hotline? Some years ago I preached a sermon called "Steering toward the Pain." I'd gone to a suicide-prevention symposium at a psychiatric center, and there was a lecture with that title. The speaker counseled all of us, when we were involved with a suicidal person, to "steer toward the pain." I understood what he meant at the time, I committed it to memory, I promised myself I would always heed that instruction. In the case of Bruce, I did not do it. I abandoned him to his despair.

Now I have also tried, off and on, to internalize another piece of advice and that is to remember that I am not the center of the world. I was not the only person in Bruce's line of sight. My failure to steer toward his pain was not the only one that he experienced that day, and in the next days and weeks. It was one of many. Nevertheless, I must acknowledge that in that one chance offered to me, I failed. I was surrounded by other social opportunities, and I steered away from his pain; and in the months that followed, I never turned back toward it.

In one person's suicide, any person's suicide, we are all involved. John Donne, perhaps the greatest preacher ever in the English language, wrote these famous words:

> No man is an island, entire of itself; every man is
> a piece of the continent, a part of the main . . . any
> man's death diminishes me, because I am involved
> in mankind; and therefore never send to know for
> whom the bell tolls; it tolls for thee.[1]

On that Good Friday outside the city walls of Jerusalem, the bell tolled for the Son of God. *Such was his involvement in mankind.* Not only did he consciously and deliberately steer toward the pain, he entered into it all the way to the bottom of despair. What he endured that day was an abandonment so great that for the first time in his human life— and even more crucially, for the first time in his divine life with the Father—he apparently felt himself to be hopelessly cut off. This sense began to overwhelm him in the Garden

1. John Donne, "Meditation 17."

of Gethsemane the night before, just an hour or so before his betrayal and arrest. The accounts in the Gospels of that struggle in the garden are striking for their emphasis on the extremity of Jesus' situation as he struggled with his destiny. Mark used the strongest language at his disposal to describe Jesus' emotion as he begged God to spare him what lay ahead. It's very important to recognize that Jesus did not beg God simply to save him from death, even such a particularly horrible death as crucifixion. No. It was the dread of submitting to the realm of Sin and Death that he feared.

We can say it even more strongly. In 2 Corinthians, Paul writes that our Lord "was made sin." It's a strange expression, to be "made sin." Two clicks on the internet will take you to all kinds of complicated disputes about what it means. I think perhaps Paul meant it to sound strange, in order to get us to pay attention. The complete verse is this: "for our sake [God] made him [Jesus] to be sin who knew no sin, so that in him we might become the righteousness of God" (2 Corinthians 5:21). This is what he experienced in the Garden of Gethsemane. When he arose from his knees he "set his face like a flint,"[2] steered toward the pain, never

2. Isaiah 50:7; see also Luke 9:51.

changed his course, and followed the path all the way down into hell. Yes, hell—the hell of being utterly abandoned by God and humanity, abandoned into the icy grip of Sin and Death, abandoned into a universe without pity, without love, without God, for ever and ever.

What is the message here for Bruce? What is the message for those of us who failed Bruce? What is the message for the people here today who are personally acquainted with the idea—or the reality—of suicide? Suicide strikes in every congregation. It has been said that despair is above all the one thing forbidden to a Christian. But sometimes the power of despair is simply too great for us without a deliverer. No one was able to be Bruce's human deliverer. Negligence, selfishness, ignorance, distractedness, laziness all played their parts—such was the drama manipulated in Bruce's life by the powers of Sin and Death.

We need to find a balance between compassion, on the one hand, and on the other hand sentimentalizing or even valorizing suicide so that people come to think of it as an act of romantic courage rather than utter desperation. Our tendermindedness, our need to put the best face on things, may not always be the most helpful course to take. A person very close to me, a devout Roman Catholic, told me years ago that she had considered suicide many times but had not gone through with it because she was afraid she would go to hell. I'm not sure that's a bad thing. To this day she struggles with the idea of suicide but resists it. Her courage is the daily struggle not to give in to the power of Death.

As you can easily imagine, I have had misgivings about this sermon and wondered if I should discard it. I have stayed with it as a signpost to the dereliction of Jesus on the cross. But is it enough to say that Jesus went through what we go through, so that he understands what we feel? I don't think so. We need to understand this in a larger way.

Hell is the absence of hope, the absence of love, the absence of light, the absence of God. On the cross, Jesus experienced the absence of God and, steering toward the pain, descended into that hell—experiencing the absolute worst. And on the third day he emerged with the battle flag of victory—**Christ the conqueror**. Light and life return with him. There is nothing, not even suicide, that can negate the victory of Christ over Death and Hell.

My prayer is that we will hear these words from Romans in that light, and in that power, today:

Who shall separate us from the love of Christ? Shall tribulation, or distress, or persecution, or famine, or nakedness, or peril, or sword? . . .

No, in all these things we are more than conquerors through him who loved us. For I am sure that neither death, nor life, nor angels, nor principalities, nor things present, nor things to come, nor powers, nor height, nor depth, nor anything else in all creation, will be able to separate us from the love of God in Christ Jesus our Lord. (Romans 8:35–39)

After this, Jesus knowing that all things were now accomplished, that the scripture might be fulfilled, saith, I thirst. Now there was set a vessel full of vinegar: and they filled a [sponge] with vinegar, and put it upon hyssop, and put it to his mouth.

John 19:28–29

The esteemed short-story writer Joy Williams wrote a book of short—and I mean *really* short—stories called *Ninety-nine Stories of God*. This one is my favorite:

The Lord was drinking some water out of a glass. There was nothing wrong with the glass, but the water tasted terrible.

This was in a white building on a vast wasteland. The engineers within wore white uniforms and bootees on their shoes and gloves on their hands. The water had traveled many hundreds of miles through wide pipes to be there.

What have you done to my water? The Lord asked. My living water . . .

Oh, they said, we thought that was just a
metaphor.[1]

In order to grasp the point here, we need to know a
passage from the Gospel of John. Jesus is on one of his long
journeys, on foot, and he comes to a town in Samaria, a
territory despised by his own people, the Jews. In the heat
of the day, he comes upon the well in the center of town,
and there is an outcast Samaritan woman there, drawing
water from the well. We know she's an outcast, because the
respectable women will be coming to the well in the cool of
the evening. So she is doubly despised, first for being a Samaritan, and second for being a loose woman. Jesus asks her
to draw water for him to drink, and she does, and then he
says to her that he has "living water," "a spring of water welling up to eternal life" (John 4:10, 14). She misunderstands,
and asks him to give her that living water so she won't have
to make the trip to the well every day.

I don't want to spoil Joy Williams's little gem of a story
by overanalyzing it. But first let's notice the twist in that
marvelous last sentence. "Oh . . . we thought that was just a

1. Joy Williams, "Wet," in *Ninety-nine Stories of God* (Portland, OR: Tin
House Books, 2016), #10.

metaphor." What a breathtaking disclosure of the way a metaphor works! A metaphor is a small word-picture that can carry vast meanings within it. When Jesus tells the woman that he can give her "living water," he's clearly speaking metaphorically, but she misses the point—she thinks he's talking about literal water from a well. The engineers in their sterile uniforms in their post-apocalypse laboratory miss the point too, only they have it backwards. They don't think Jesus' water applies to real drinking water. "Just a metaphor." This is the height of irony, but the irony leads us further into the way biblical language works. The scientists in their sterile labs have heard the story of the Samaritan woman, and they have airily dismissed it. In Joy Williams's little dystopian tale, we can imagine that there are unimaginable numbers of people dead somewhere. The idea seems to be that some kind of environmental disaster has occurred, and the engineers have water piped in from great distances, apparently not caring about the human significance of this. We might think of the city government in Flint, Michigan, who ignored the evidence that people with little political voice or agency were being poisoned by the local water. Perhaps some of the officials were churchgoers who never thought to wonder if there might be some analogy between

Jesus' living water and literal drinking water. So there's a double layer of meaning here, early in the Gospel of John, that will reappear at the climax of the story of Jesus' passion and death.

On Good Friday, when the afternoon drew on, the Fourth Evangelist tells us, the religious authorities went to Pilate, the Roman governor, and asked that the crucified men have their legs broken so they would die faster. This was because they didn't want to leave Jesus' body on the cross on the Sabbath. As the Torah says, a body left hanging on a tree is cursed by God (Deuteronomy 21:23). Did you get that? Cursed by God. St. Paul fastened on that idea in his letter to the Galatians (Galatians 3:13). So the religious men got permission, and the Roman soldiers came to break the legs of the men on the crosses, so they would die faster. Jesus, however, had already died, so they did not break his legs ("not a bone of him shall be broken"—John is quoting Psalm 34:20). Instead, one soldier thrust a spear into his side ("they shall look on him whom they have pierced"— John quotes Zechariah 12:10) and out of the wound flowed blood and water (John 19:34). From earliest times, Christian interpreters have understood this as the sacrificial blood of the communion cup, and the water as the living symbol of baptism. Thus in this one brief detail in the story, we see the death of Jesus as the origin and source of the river of life given to the church in its sacraments. Early in John's narrative, the Lord says to the Samaritan woman that he gives a "spring of water welling up to eternal life" (John 4:14), but we don't understand this metaphor until his hour comes— his hour of being lifted up on the cross—so that the water from his side becomes "a stream of blessing and salvation."[2]

There are layers of meaning here, all pointing to one truth. No human being can live more than two or three days without anything to drink. That's the factual reality. So we're not just talking about metaphorical water here. The Samaritan in John's story is enslaved by her own appetites and her subsequent isolation, but she is nevertheless dependent upon coming to the well for water. When Jesus meets her, we are told, he is weary from his long walk in the heat of the sun. The Lord has taken full human nature upon himself and experiences weakness just like us. Thirst is perhaps the ultimate human weakness; we can do without food for a while, but not water. I can't say that I have ever experienced extreme thirst. Perhaps some of you have. I've heard that

2. Rudolf Schnackenburg, *The Gospel according to St. John* (New York: Crossroad, 1982), 3:293.

it is uniquely terrible. The gift of a cup of water in Mark's Gospel is held up as the epitome of response to human need: "For truly, I say to you, whoever gives you a cup of water to drink because you bear the name of Christ, will by no means lose his reward" (Mark 9:41). Yet when Jesus was nailed to the cross no one gave him so much as a single sip of water.

I wonder what brought you off the streets of the city into this sanctuary today. I wonder if there are some here who do not really understand what we are doing, taking off an hour, or three hours, to worship a man who died most horribly, more horribly than most of us dare to imagine, and not only died horribly but died in shame, forsaken, derided, outcast, unable to lift a finger to help himself. What is he doing there? Why do we come today? There will be many more people here on Sunday than there are today, yet those of you here today—a goodly number of you, actually—have come, or have been led by some power greater than yourselves, to the very heart and center of our Christian faith. Who is this man who is tormented, not only by extreme pain and utter degradation, but also by the most elemental form of bodily desperation—to die of thirst like a nameless migrant expiring alone in the desert along the border? Yes,

in this death that he freely chooses, Jesus comes alongside
the least and the lost of humanity. Even the most basic, most
elemental human comfort is denied him. I beg you to think
about this. There are three men on crosses that day. All of
them are in prolonged agony. All of them are suffering extreme thirst. Why should the historian bother to record the
fact that Jesus said he was thirsty? According to the Scriptures, he was fully human in the most fundamental sense.
If, in his incarnate life, Jesus had drunk the water in Flint,
Michigan, he also would have been poisoned just like us.
He was completely vulnerable on the cross. He needed *real
water*, not metaphorical water, and no one gave him any. It is
the remarkable imagination of Joy Williams that permits us
to see the intricate connection between *actual water*—pure
mountain streams, great lakes and seas, vast oceans, all of it
created by God, *all of it endangered* by the carelessness and
greed of humankind—and the *living water* of eternal life in
Jesus Christ.

Until his crucifixion, we don't fully see that Jesus Christ
himself *is* the wellspring of the river of eternal life. I have
often been upstate to Cooperstown, and I always go to see
the headwaters of the Susquehanna. It is marvelous to me to
see where that beautiful river rises on its four-hundred-mile

journey to the ocean. I have read books about the nine-teenth-century explorers' journeys to find the mysterious source of the Nile River—it makes very exciting reading. It's human nature to want to find and marvel at the source of rivers. Well, Jesus the Son of God is the Source of the river of the water of life. In the last book of the New Testament, the Revelation to St. John the Divine, we see the vision of the City of God, and Jesus, "the Lamb of God who takes away the sin of the world," is enthroned there, and we behold the vision of

> the river of the water of life, bright as crystal, flowing from the throne of God and of the Lamb through the middle of the street of the city; also, on either side of the river, the tree of life . . . and the leaves of the tree were for the healing of the nations. There shall no more be anything accursed, but the throne of God and of the Lamb shall be in it, and his servants shall worship him; they shall see his face, and his name shall be on their foreheads. And night shall be no more; they need no light of lamp or sun, for the Lord God will be their light, and they shall reign for ever and ever. (Revelation 22:1–5)

So the water from Jesus' side, together with the lifegiving blood of the Lamb, is the metaphor for the eternal life that God gives to our human race, our race that seems more than ever to be bent on destroying itself and its beautiful planet. The interplay here between symbolism and factual reality is endlessly rich. Human beings cannot live without water. In the age to come, in the city of God that will come down from heaven, there is a river of unquenchable love, bought for us by the agony and thirst of the only-begotten Son of God. Come to his water. Come to his cross. Come to his blood, shed for you . . . and find for yourselves the gift of the love that will never fail.

Now there was set a vessel full of vinegar: and they filled a [sponge] with vinegar, and put it upon hyssop, and put it to his mouth. When Jesus therefore had received the vinegar, he said, It is finished: and he bowed his head, and gave up the ghost.

John 19:29–30

E ach of the four evangelists—Matthew, Mark, Luke, John—each one has his own particular way of framing the story of Jesus' passion and death. Each one wants to tell us in the most convincing way possible that the crucifixion of the Son of God is the most important thing that has ever happened and that it reveals the true and complete destiny of humanity and the creation. In this pause, here in this sanctuary, we have come together to reflect on these four collections of the living memories of Jesus. Any four people composing a long narrative will have four different ways of putting it across—what to emphasize, what to leave out, how to bring it to a conclusion. Each of the four has done his work painstakingly in order to convey in the most arresting terms the profound, world-overthrowing significance of the crucifixion of Jesus. The accounts of Mark and Matthew, though they differ from each other in ways that greatly enrich us, have one crucial feature in common: both of them have only one saying, and it's the same one: "My God, my God, why have you forsaken me?" As we saw in an earlier hour, it is a cry of dereliction—more like a shriek than a cry—a shriek of utmost abandonment. We reflected on this despairing shriek earlier in these three hours. On the cross, Jesus the Messiah experienced hell, the absence of God, the ultimate judgment—and in so doing appeared to suffer ultimate defeat at the hands of the Evil One, the demonic usurper, the Power set against God and against all that God created. Both Mark and Matthew shape their passion narratives to highlight this one saying. They want us to know that there is no hell that Jesus has not entered, no demon that he has not confronted, no abandonment or despair that he has not felt. He experienced the great nihilistic swallowing up of all goodness. Mark and Matthew both emphasize this aspect of the passion narrative.

The Gospel of John tells the same story another way. We need to pay attention to each of the Gospels separately in order fully to understand what they want us to know. John's Good Friday narrative incorporates three sayings that were treasured by him and his community. John ends his passion story with these words of Jesus: "It is finished."

I'm sure I'm not the only person who always thought this meant, "It's over" . . . "It's the end." Certainly that's what I thought when I was a young person hearing the story. But I soon came to understand that the saying means infinitely more than that. The root word in Greek is *telos*. It means, simply, "end," which would certainly suggest that Jesus was saying, "The end has come, it's all over." But that is not at all what the word *telos* means in John. John emphasizes all through his Gospel that Jesus is never the passive victim. He is not on the cross by mistake. He is not, as we so often say, just "the wrong person in the wrong place at the wrong time." The crucifixion is not just an unfortunate thing that happened to Jesus on his way to the resurrection. It is not a momentary blip on the arc of his ascent to the Father. John tells us otherwise. It is precisely *on the cross that the work of Jesus is carried through to its completion.*

What then is the resurrection? It is the vindication of the crucified One. The resurrection doesn't cancel out the crucifixion as if it were only a passing episode to be noted briefly (or not) on the way to Easter. You here today are blessed because you know, or you have suspected, that Good Friday is not optional. You understand, or you are on the way to understanding, that the Day of Resurrection finds its meaning from the cross. The resurrection does not *reverse* the crucifixion. The resurrection *vindicates* the crucifixion (vindicate, meaning to verify, confirm, authenticate). The work of Jesus is brought to completion *on the cross*. That's what "it is finished" means. The Father and the Son together, in the power of the Spirit, are saying to us, the work that the Father gave the Son to accomplish is consummated, completed, finished *as he dies*. The saying is just one word in Greek: *tetelestai*. The Latin is particularly good: *consummatum est*. So you see, the resurrection does not cancel out the cross. It verifies and confirms that the cross was the main event.

If we go back two verses in John's passion narrative, we read that directly after Jesus brings his new community into being with the saying "Woman, behold your son," *immediately after that* Jesus knew "that all was now finished" (*tetelestai*) (John 19:28). "All was now finished." Same word twice in two verses. That is very emphatic! There are many threads in John's Gospel that are being tied together here in the word *tetelestai*, finished. The life-work of Christ is brought to its consummation. He has fulfilled the Scripture. To all who receive him, he has given power to become children of God (John 1:12). He has offered himself as the Lamb of God who takes away the sin of the world. He has created the new community, the church.

And he does this in full knowledge of his true Enemy. Charles Spurgeon, the towering nineteenth-century preacher, adds to our understanding of Christ's whole life as a battle with the demonic powers under the command of "the ruler of this world." These forces have only one purpose: to destroy the mission of the Son of God. Spurgeon evokes a breathtaking image of Jesus on the cross as a great champion in a mighty contest with Satan. This is exactly what Jesus himself says at the turning point of John's narrative: "'The hour has come. . . . Now . . . shall the ruler of this world be cast out; and I, when I am lifted up from the earth, will draw all [humanity] to myself.' He said this to show by what death he was to die" (John 12:23, 31–33).

You see? He knows what he has come to accomplish. He will create a new humanity, but in order to do so he must first engage and dislodge the Enemy in battle—the "ruler of this world." He will do this precisely *on the cross*. He will accomplish his work as the sacrificial Lamb of God. Twice in the first chapter of John, Jesus is called "the Lamb of God, who takes away the sin of the world" (John 1:29, 36). How and when will he do this? In his redeeming and atoning death.

In John's Gospel, Jesus prepares his disciples for all of this at the Last Supper. "When Jesus knew that his hour had come to depart out of this world to the Father, having loved his own who were in the world, he loved them to the end [*eis telos*]" (John 13:1). After the meal is finished and Judas Iscariot has departed to do his treacherous deed, Jesus says to the disciples who remain,

> I will no longer talk much with you, for the ruler of this world is coming. He has no power over me; but I do as the Father has commanded me, so that the world may know that I love the Father. Rise, let us go hence. (John 14:30–31)

"The ruler of this world is coming." The Father and the Son are acting with a single will to enter into the final battle with Satan. The battle takes place on the cross. Jesus places himself in the direct path of the forces of evil arrayed against him in hand-to-hand conflict. He appears to lose the battle. But even as he dies, he is already the victor. He passes his laurels to his new community, represented by his mother and the disciple standing at his feet. Like a champion having overcome his foes he shouts, "It is finished!" The will of God has been accomplished.

None of this—nothing of what we have said, sung, and heard—makes any sense whatsoever unless Jesus Christ is who the Scriptures say he is. Here are his own words in John's Gospel. He is speaking to the questioning disciple Philip, who has asked him, "Lord, show us the Father." Jesus says,

> Have I been with you so long, and yet you do not know me, Philip? He who has seen me has seen the Father; how can you say, "Show us the Father"? Do you not believe that I am [*ego en*] in the Father and the Father in me? (John 14:9–10)

On another occasion he says,

> I and the Father are one. (John 10:30)

Three hours is no time at all when we consider the glory and majesty of Jesus Christ. The preacher is very limited, not only in time but in ability. All the same, there is no better way to tell you what the preacher is attempting to do on Good Friday than to read to you the words of John the Evangelist near the end of his Gospel. John writes that Jesus did many signs and showed himself in many other ways than he has written about in his book, "but these are written [and these sermons are preached] that you may [come to] believe that Jesus is the Christ, the Son of God, and that believing you may have life in his name" (John 20:30–31).

And it was about the sixth hour, and there was a darkness over all the earth until the ninth hour. And the sun was darkened, and the veil of the temple was rent in the midst. And when Jesus had cried with a loud voice, he said, Father, into thy hands I commend my spirit: and having said thus, he gave up the ghost.

Luke 23:44–46

For those who have joined us along the way, I have been making the point that the four Gospels, while sharing all essentials in common, differ from one another in many respects, and a careful look at some of these differences can greatly enrich us. The accounts of Mark and Matthew have a particular feature in common, of exceptional importance. Unlike Luke and John, which each have three sayings unique to them, Matthew and Mark have only one saying, and it is the same one. As we saw in an earlier hour, it is the cry of dereliction—more like a shriek than a cry—a shriek of utmost abandonment. I do not like to think what we would have lost without "My God, my God, why have you forsaken me?" If we did not have this saying, our understanding of what the Lord has done for us in his ghastly death would be fatally impoverished. It is the cry of dereliction that confirms for us the depths to which the Son of

God descended for our sake and in our place, that we might
be delivered from the worst that could possibly happen. We
may truly affirm that Jesus Christ entered into hell in order
to deliver us from evil.

And so we come to the final saying of Jesus from the
cross in Luke's Gospel. The three sayings in Luke are softer
than those in the other accounts. Jesus speaks of forgiveness, of paradise in his presence, and now he gives himself
into his Father's hands. We are not to prefer one Gospel's
sayings over another's; it is the fullness of them all that we
need to receive. But it is helpful to hear each Evangelist's
testimony from its own perspective, like turning a prism to
catch different colors and patterns. The traditional order
of the sayings, hallowed by long use, places this one last in
the series of seven: "Father, into thy hands I commend my
spirit" (Luke 23:46).

I have long cherished something said to me by a person
in great pain. He was Paul Lehmann, my mentor, profes-
sor of theological ethics, a man of towering intellect and
dazzling imagination, to whom I remained close throughout
the last three decades of his life. He and his wife suffered
the loss of their only child, the son of their middle age—a
loss for which there was to be no compensation in this life. I

spent much time with him and his grieving wife in subsequent years. He taught me, in words and example, that the life of a Christian is lived in the tension between "My God, my God, why hast thou forsaken me?" and "Father, into thy hands I commend my spirit." That, perhaps, is the message above all that we can take with us out into the unheeding city this afternoon. What does it mean to live between those two sayings of Jesus from the cross, sayings that seem so contradictory?

The evangelist Luke has generally been beloved for several reasons: the nativity story unique to his Gospel; his emphasis on the healings of Jesus and his relationships with women; the special parables like those of the prodigal son and the good Samaritan. It is tempting to be a little sentimental about Luke. That would be a mistake. Here is a passage from Luke's account of a major turning point in Jesus' ministry. It's a rare passage, for most of Jesus' teaching is very grounded, very earthy—but in this unusual moment he has an apocalyptic vision, and he describes it to his little group of disciples: "I saw Satan fall like lightning from heaven" (Luke 10:18). We therefore know that he had before him the vision of his victory. In this, Luke is like John. In John, the Fourth Gospel, as the hour of Jesus' death approaches, Jesus

says, "Now is the judgment of this world, now shall the ruler
of this world be cast out" (John 12:31). Luke and John both
share in the cosmology of all the New Testament writers,
that human life is lived on a battlefield between God and
God's great Enemy, "the ruler of this world," also called Satan
and, by Jesus in John's Gospel, "the father of lies." Lesslie
Newbigin, the great missionary theologian of the Church of
South India, put it all into one sentence:

> The deepest motive for mission is simply to be with
> Jesus where he is, on the frontier between the reign
> of God and the usurped dominion of the devil.[1]

That is pure New Testament theology, having everything to do with living life on the edge, between this age
of Sin and Death and the Age to Come. Did we think that
forgiving his enemies on the cross came easily to our Lord
because he was the Son of God? Did we think that bringing
the bandit on the cross into paradise was a smooth transi-
tion into the beyond? Earlier Jesus had said to his disciples,
"As the lightning flashes and lights up the sky from one side

---

1. Lesslie Newbigin, *A Word in Season* (Grand Rapids: Eerdmans, 1994), 129.

to the other, so will the Son of man be in his day. But first he must suffer many things and be rejected" (Luke 17:24–25). His triumph would be won, but only at greatest cost. Once, we are told, "while they were all marveling" at the wonderful things he did—the healings and exorcisms and miracles— he turned to them and said, abruptly, "Let these words sink into your ears; for the Son of man is to be delivered into the hands of [wicked] men" (Luke 9:44).

So the New Testament teaching is clear about the conditions in which we must live. The Christian life is a struggle against the powers of Sin and Death. At the time of V-E (Victory in Europe) Day, 1945, J. R. R. Tolkien along with many other Europeans had gone through two world wars. He himself had been in the infamously terrible battle of the Somme in World War I. In one of his personal letters at the end of the second war, he wrote:

> It all seems rather a mockery to me, for the War is not over. . . . But it is of course wrong to fall into such a mood, for Wars are always lost, and The War always goes on; and it is no good growing faint![2]

2. *The Letters of J. R. R. Tolkien* (Boston: Houghton Mifflin, 2000), 115–16. Pope John Paul II said something similar, years later: "War is always a defeat

No good growing faint. That is a fine rallying call, but for most of us it is almost impossible to maintain vigilance over a long period of time—say, over a lifetime. Yet vigilance is a major theme of the Bible, which comes into particular prominence during the season of Advent. Watchfulness for the signs of the Kingdom of God in the midst of tribulation is one of the chief characteristics of the Christian life. We cannot maintain this sort of balance without divine aid. It is for this purpose that the Son of God became incarnate, to fight alongside us in our battles, however humdrum they may seem. The people whom Jesus drew into his orbit were no great heroic characters. They became heroes of faith only very gradually and not without much conflict—"fightings and fears within, without."[3] I remember reading years ago about the Anglican Dean of Johannesburg, Gonville ffrench-Beytagh, who was active in the resistance to apartheid in South Africa, condemning it publicly as "blasphemous against God and man."[4] He was arrested, held in soli-

---

for humanity" (annual address to diplomatic representatives, Vatican City, January 13, 2003).

3. Paul's words in 2 Corinthians 7:5 were metrically shaped thus for the hymn "Just As I Am" by Charlotte Elliott (1789–1871).

4. "In Retrospect: Canon Gonville Aubie ffrench-Beytagh (1912–1991),"

tary confinement, and brutally interrogated. He was a fragile man, not at all in the heroic mold, and he spoke later of his weakness in prison. Yet he entered the struggle knowingly, aware of exactly what he was up against.

In all four Gospels we see Jesus Christ engaged in a struggle to the death with the enemy Powers occupying God's created order. His first action in Mark's Gospel is to confront and drive out a demon. At the time and place of Jesus' crucifixion, Satan is given free rein to enlist the whole human race in sadistic action against the Son of God. That is part of what the cry of dereliction signifies. At the same time, the last saying in Luke, such a contrast to the cry of abandonment, preserves for the faithful Christian the guarantee that life lived in this tension between utter desolation and faithful trust is not only possible but in fact is the place where we will most certainly find our Lord and Master. We learn from him the right way to position ourselves for the duration of our lives. The two sayings taken together, the cry of dereliction and the last giving over to the Father's care, "meet in the *mysterium* of

---

available at http://www.patrickcomerford.com/2012/04/in-retrospect-canon-gonville-aubie.html.

Jesus' person, and both reveal something to us of the secret of our own death."[5]

In one of her essays, Flannery O'Connor wrote, "The creative action of the Christian's life is to prepare his death in Christ."[6] Those of you who are younger may find this off-putting, but even when I was decades younger than I am now, I found the thought of my own death *in Christ* curiously strengthening. Paradoxically, it gives somehow a zest for life. It's as though the knowledge of his presence in our death is exactly what we need to rejoice in the life he gives without fear of its ending. As T. S. Eliot wrote, "In my end is my beginning."[7]

Our time together is drawing to a close. I think any preacher who goes through the Three Hours must feel that his or her words are very feeble in comparison with their incomparable subject. And yet one feels a great responsibility toward you, whose faces I can see in these pews. Those of you who have been here for all three hours—and there

5. Schnackenburg, *The Gospel according to St. John*, 3:285. This is not a Lukan commentary, obviously, but the Johannine scholar's statement makes the point with imagination and depth.

6. Flannery O'Connor, *Mystery and Manners* (New York: Farrar, Straus and Giroux, 1969), 223.

7. T. S. Eliot, *Four Quartets* (New York: Harcourt, Brace, 1943), 32.

seem to have been quite a few of you—have stayed with our Lord on the cross for some special reason. The Father of Jesus has his hand on you in some way. You can trust that. You can give yourself up in this hour to the prayer of our Redeemer, and commit yourself into our Father's hands *through him*. Our final hymn is a gift enabling you to do that. The words are utterly simple, and they say everything we need to confess today.

> Here the King of all the ages,
> Throned in light ere worlds could be,
> Robed in mortal flesh is dying,
> Crucified by sin for me.[8]

8. "Cross of Jesus, Cross of Sorrow," hymn by William J. Sparrow-Simpson (1860–1952), sung to the tune *Cross of Jesus* by John Stainer.